IRONWORK:
DYNAMIC DETAILS

Dona Z. Meilach

4880 Lower Valley Road, Atglen, PA 19310 USA

I am pleased to dedicate this book to
Russell Jaqua
for his vision, his legacy, his sculpture, and his enduring contribution
to the field of modern artist-blacksmithing.

OTHER ART-CRAFT BOOKS
By DONA Z. MEILACH
METAL WORKING/BLACKSMITHING
Ironwork Today Inside & Out
The Contemporary Blacksmith
Decorative & Sculptural Ironwork
Architectural Ironwork
Fireplace Accessories
Direct Metal Sculpture
Also:
Wood Art Today
Art Jewelry Today
Teapots, Makers & Collectors
Contemporary Stone Sculpture
Creating Modern Furniture
and others

Copyright © 2007 by Dona Z . Meilach
Library of Congress Control Number: 2006929316

Designed by Dona Z. Meilach
Layout by "Sue"
Type set in Swis721 Blk BT/Humanst521 BT

ISBN: 0-7643-2549-3
Printed in China

Published by Schiffer Publishing Ltd.
4880 Lower Valley Road
Atglen, PA 19310
Phone: (610) 593-1777; Fax: (610) 593-2002
E-mail: Info@schifferbooks.com

For the largest selection of fine reference books on this and related subjects, please visit our web site at
www.schifferbooks.com
We are always looking for people to write books on new and related subjects. If you have an idea for a book please contact us at the above address.

This book may be purchased from the publisher.
Include $3.95 for shipping.
Please try your bookstore first.
You may write for a free catalog.

In Europe, Schiffer books are distributed by
Bushwood Books
6 Marksbury Ave.
Kew Gardens
Surrey TW9 4JF England
Phone: 44 (0) 20 8392-8585; Fax: 44 (0) 20 8392-9876
E-mail: info@bushwoodbooks.co.uk
Website: www.bushwoodbooks.co.uk
Free postage in the U.K., Europe; air mail at cost.

Contents

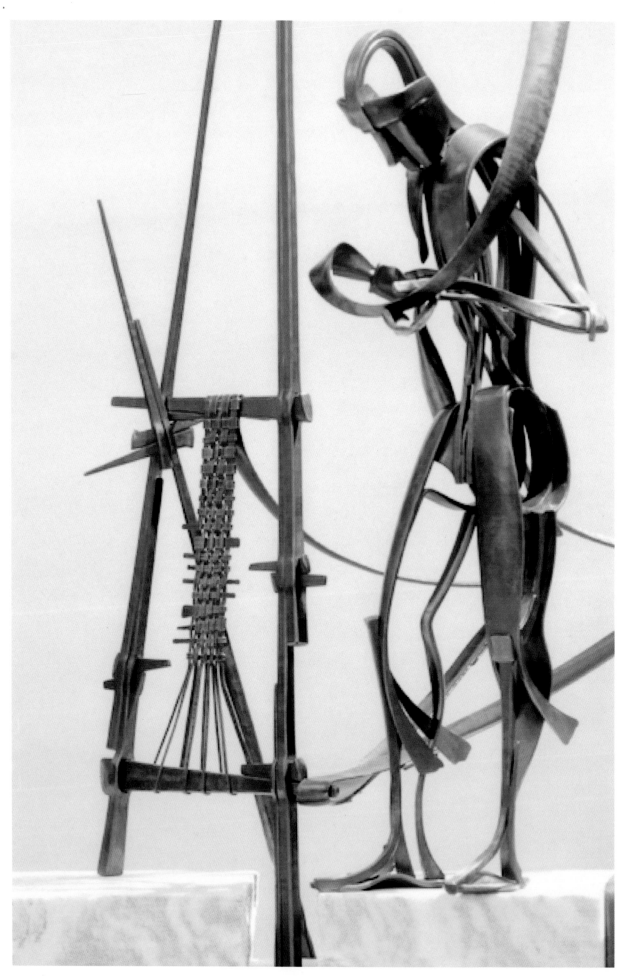

Daniel Miller. *In Wind We Woven Weave.* Detail of a sculpture. Steel. *Photo, Steve Keull*

Preface & Acknowledgments

This book is the result of dismay and delight. While poring through photos for my last book, *Ironwork Today Inside & Out*, I was dismayed by how much work could not be used because the photos were not up to publication quality or because there wasn't adequate room even for the good photos. It is not easy to photograph installed fences and railings with distracting extraneous objects, inadequate lighting, or poor photographic abilities. But looking at those rejected photos made me realize that good photos could be achieved for close-up details. Often the details were as exciting as the whole piece, or helped to make the piece unique.

Therefore, I requested artists to send me photographs of details; portions of gates, doors, railings, anything that the artist felt was so unique and well done that it could almost stand as a work of art by itself. And with the increased use of digital photography it was easy to isolate portions of a photograph and fix lighting that was not quite up to par for publication. As details came in, I was delighted with the results and I believe that you will be, too.

It was Katherine Kagler's stylized flower details that alerted me to the possibility of a book dealing only with details, and I have used several of her pieces in this book as well as in *Ironwork Today Inside & Out*. John Boyd Smith's photos were a veritable treasure trove of details, and wherever I needed another example to round out a theme, I could rely on his vast and varied output and his wife's excellent photography. Helmut Hillenkamp also provided photographs of his own work and of pieces in the Santa Fe, New Mexico, area by different artists. He kindly took time to read portions of the manuscript. My thanks to all the artists and photographers who graciously submitted many more photos than the number you will see in the following pages.

Dona Z. Meilach
Carlsbad, California

Chapter 1

Flowers and Nature

Ever since mankind began forming metal into shapes, he looked to nature for ideas. People usually associate ironwork with fences and railings, and have a mental picture of upright straight and twisted bars and, perhaps some shaped in curves with a few scrolls. However, ironwork can include an infinite variety of shapes and imagery including medallions, flowers, fruits, and leaves as dominant design elements.

Early traditional ironwork often included acanthus leaves attached to scroll endings. Sometimes leaves were made of copper, or gilded with leaf gold for a decorative contrast to the black iron. In England, France, and Italy, entire gates and fences were often gilded.

When the term artist-blacksmith inched into the lexicon, a generation of young people was becoming intrigued by the versatility of iron. Many were trained as artists, often having developed three-dimensional forms in other materials. When they began working iron they brought along their artistic visions and began forming metal into new shapes that were expressive as well as decorative. New tools, welding techniques, and easier to use equipment helped further and popularize the art form.

The floral details shown in this chapter may be made of steel, copper, bronze, or other metals. Flowers may look realistic, they may be stylized, abstract, or purely the figment of the artist's imagination. But they are all inspired by nature. Some are small and may be only a few inches long and an element among many others on a gate, a door, a sconce, a chandelier, or they may be large as in the public sculpture of sunflowers by Jeff Fetty. They may be left in their natural iron color and allowed to rust, or they can be painted or patinated. The potential is unending.

Left:
Andrew Chambers. Wrought iron calla lily railing detail forged and fabricated. Clear powder coat finish. *Photo, Stacey Chambers*

Katherine Kagler. *Lickum.* A stylized flower detail with a pea vine stamen. *Photo, artist*

Left:
Katherine Kagler. Heavily textured elements in a decorative garden grille. The flower stems are forged into traditional wraps that attach the flowers to the scrollwork. *Photo, artist*

Nikolay Semenov. Showing the construction of a flower back used for a stair railing. *Photo, artist*

John Monteath and Brenda Field. Floral elements as part of a stair railing. *Photo, artist*

Stefan Duerst. Lily blossom positioned at the top of a garden gate. *Photo, artist*

George Witzke. Morning glories of steel with copper tendrils used for a lamp base. *Photo, April Witzke*

Katherine Kagler. Nasturtium showing the interior curling pistil. In some of the flowers, the exterior rotates. *Photo, artist*

Sergey Sakirkin. A flower for a stair railing molded and shaped from one piece of steel. *Photo, artist*

Stefan Duerst. Lily, closed, atop a garden gate. *Photo, artist*

Sergey Sakirkin. Flower for a stair railing molded and shaped from one piece of steel and riveted to the railing. *Photo, artist*

Jim Holahan. The sunflower is a subject for myriad applications and varied design and style interpretations by artist-blacksmiths. This one, with a colored glass inset, is used on a drapery rod. 4.5" diam. *Photo, artist*

Nikolay Semenov and Egor Bavykin. Abstract leaf with rivets are a repeated theme in the St. Nikolay Chapel gate, Odessa. *Photo, Semenov*

Susan Madacsi. *Dahlia* – back view, above. Front view, below. *Photos, R. J. Phil*

Helmut Hillenkamp. Rose buds used outdoors on various sites including gates, lattices, and entry light sconces. *Photo, artist*

Debra Turner. Sunflowers on a Tuscan-theme birdbath. Raw steel purposely left to rust in the garden. *Photo, Eric Montgomery*

The size and floppiness of sunflower petals make them a fitting inspiration for the metalworker.

Rob Gardner and Eric Velleca. Flower with a hummingbird is a garden gate detail in forged bronze. *Photo, Ken Nelson*

Rob Gardner and Eric Velleca. Flower caught in its opening stage.
Detail for a garden gate. Forged bronze. *Photo, Ken Nelson*

Butch Lee. Tulip details for an outdoor railing. *Photo, David Harres*

John Boyd Smith. Hydrangea. *Photo, Rhonda Neil Fleming*

John Boyd Smith. Wild flower. *Photo, Rhonda Neil Fleming*

Nikolay Semenov. Abstract flower and bud with wide collaring as part of a door and grille for a church, *Photo, artist*

Nikolay Semenov. Abstract flower and banding details for the end of a banister *Photo, artist*

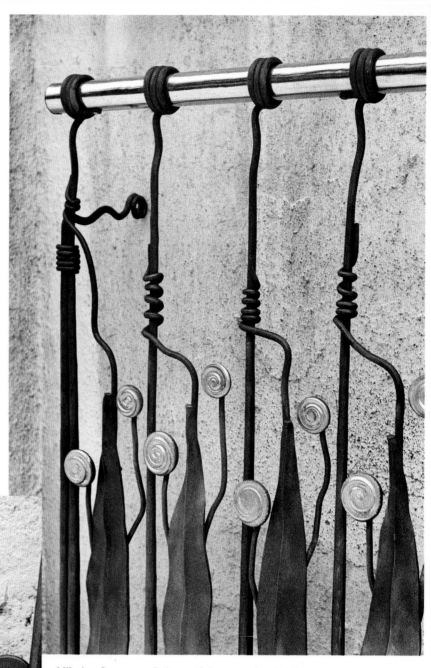

Nikolay Semenov. Railing with leaves and coiled flowers. *Photo, artist*

Nikolay Semenov. Back side of leaves and coiled flowers. *Photo, artist*

Rob Gardner and Eric Velleca. Flowers, leaves, and buds of forged bronze as part of a cocktail table base. *Photo, Ken Nelson*

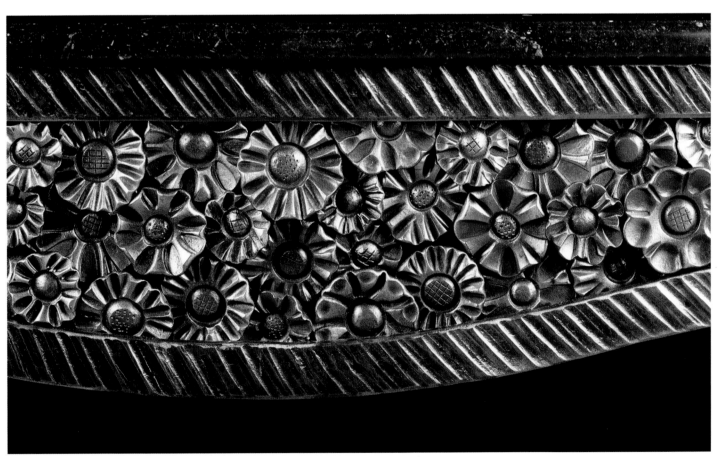

Jeff Fetty. Stylized hand-forged flower rosettes fill the apron of a console table. Of the more than 100 rosettes no two are the same. *Photo, Jim Osborn*

Robert C. Bentley. A cornucopia of acrylic painted metal flowers arranged in a half round copper basket and attached to the face of a passage gate at The Villa Toscana, Paso Robles, California. *Photo, Bruce Woodworth*

Robert C. Bentley. A colorful acrylic painted bouquet of steel flowers in a copper hanging basket for a gate at The Villa Toscana, Paso Robles, California. *Photo. Bruce Woodworth*

Debra Turner. Copper roses with steel stems. *Photo, Eric Montgomery*

Nick Swanson. Roses of iron and copper. *Photo, Neil Mansfield*

Cody Taylor. Aster of iron and copper. *Photo, Neil Mansfield*

Michael Morin. Sunflower of iron and copper. *Photo, Neil Mansfield*

Elizabeth Brim. Euphrasia made for the trim on a hat that is actually a sculpture. (Below.) *Photos, Tom Mills*

Bottom
Larry Crawford. Stylized flower on a fireplace screen. *Photo, Brenda Ladd*

John Boyd Smith.
Sunflower from a
sunflower gate. *Photo,
Rhonda Neil Fleming*

John Boyd Smith.
Wild flower from a
wild flower gate.
*Photo, Rhonda Neil
Fleming*

George Witzke. Painted steel morning glories for a fence. *Photo, April Witzke*

Katherine Kagler. Hibiscus with stamen detail formed using an oxy-acetylene torch to apply dots of filler metal. *Photo, artist*

Jeff Fetty. Coffee table with nature theme using blossoms forged from 18" plate. The legs are heavily textured and the rocks on the bottom are forged from 1" x 4" x 4" steel blocks. *Photo, Gefeti*

Dennis Dusek. Flowers. Steel with a bronze patina. *Photo, Steve Sugar*

John Boyd Smith. Banana and palm leaves for a room divider in a Florida hotel. *Photo, Rhonda Nell Fleming*

Dietrich Hoecht. Detail of a lampshade made of bent bronze rods and copper wire. The steel leaves have been colored with enamels. Copper bluish patinated round mushroom caps and a dogwood blossom are mixed in with the leaves. *Photo, artist*

Frank Jackson. Iris of forged iron. A 13" high sculpture modeled while looking at an iris in bloom. *Photo, Tim Fleming*

Nature's iris as inspiration.

Jeff Fetty. Iris finished with brass brushing on hot metal. *Photo, Gefeti*

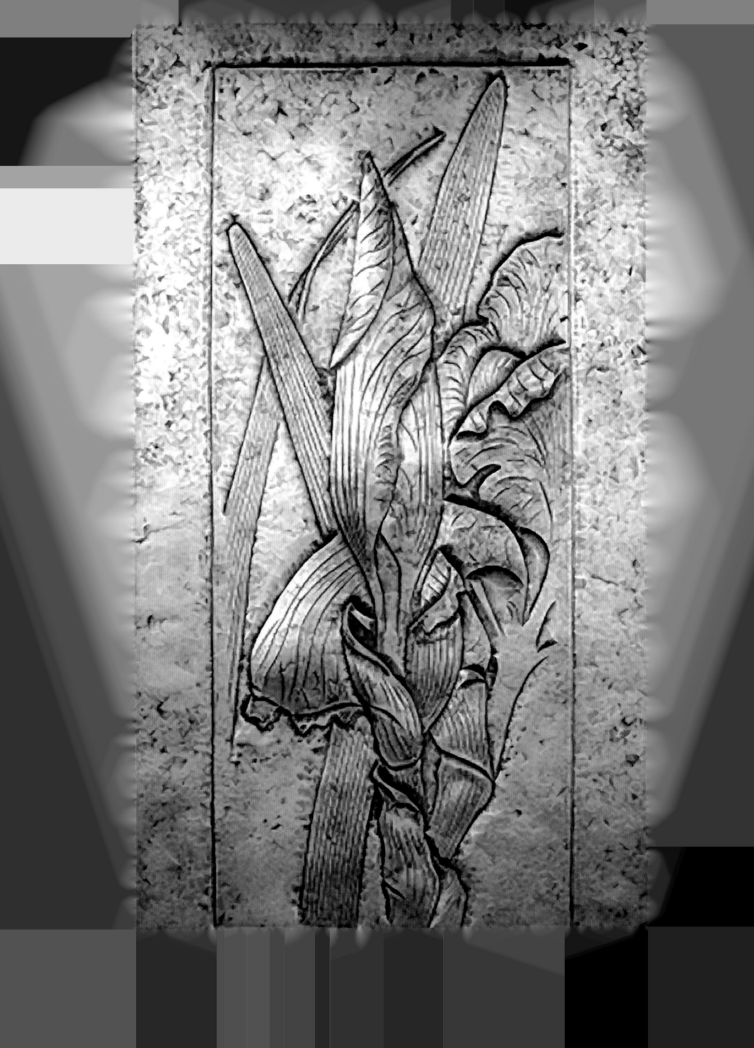

Mindy Gardner. Close-up detail of the iris bud shows the rich texture resulting from chasing and other repoussé techniques.

Left:
Mindy Gardner. Iris bud. Chasing and repoussé of 12-gauge mild steel. Oil and wax finish. *Photos, artist*

Jeff Fetty. Roses, stems, leaves, and vines for a table base. *Photo, Gefeti*

John Boyd Smith. Sunburst on a Spanish Revival style rail. *Photo, Rhonda Neil Fleming*

Helmut Hillenkamp. Iron hammered into shapes representing a kelp forest for a room divider. *Photo, artist*

Helmut Hillenkamp. *Strange bird.* Bird of paradise on a railing in a private residence, New York. The idea for this shape was taken from a wallpaper stencil used around the turn of the century, interpreted into iron, and then a new wallpaper stencil was made to shadow the ironwork. Collaboration with designer Joanne De Palma. *Photo, artist*

Robert Wiederrick. Roses used in the corners of a fireplace screen. *Photo, Michelle Wiederrick*

Robert Wiederrick. Flower with scroll used on the four corners of a fireplace screen. *Photo, Michelle Wiederrick*

Robert Wiederrick. Edelweiss flower at the corners of a fireplace screen. *Photo, Michelle Wiederrick*

Nick Wellenstein. Fireplace with acorns and oak leaves, on a fireplace screen. *Photo, artist*

Robert Wiederrick. Pine cones from a fireplace screen. *Photo, Michelle Wiederrick*

39

Rouel Darling, Nick Rinehart, and Albert Prunz. Wheat sheaves with iron "rope" for bundling used on a driveway double gate. *Photo, Jodie Darling*

Below:
John Boyd Smith. Scottish thistle. Study for a railing. *Photo, Rhonda Neil Fleming*

Jeff Fetty. Details of a giant flower garden outdoors sculpture. *Photo, Gefeti*

Chapter 2

Grapes, Vines, and Leaves

Nature supplies the inspiration for countless ironwork applications. Flowers, shown in chapter 1, test the sculptural ability of the artist-blacksmith. Grapes, vines, and leaves are among the popular nature inspired subjects.

Emulating nature's grape harvest is no easy task. Each grape must be hand formed, and each artist-blacksmith uses whatever works best for the purpose. Some will shape each half of the grape into a die. Soft metals can be hammered into the die to make a half round, and then the 2 halves are welded together. The seam must be smoothed, the form polished, painted, or patinated for the final coloring.

Other methods include beginning with a large ball bearing, heating it, hammering and shaping it. Still another is to begin with a steel rod, heat one end and shape it in a rounded die. The other end is forged to become the stem. Additional grapes are made from the rod and welded to form a cluster. Leaves may be attached. Mass produced grape clusters may be cast from an original.

Vines made of metal rod must be textured and shaped and the grapes gathered into a cluster and attached to the vines. Leaves may be added.

Why are grapes so popular? They are symbolic of wine; and the wine industry is so vast that grapes become an identifying symbol. Individuals who collect and appreciate fine wines also use the symbol for details in their homes. It is not unusual to find grapes on fences, doors, handles, gates, railings, light fixtures, and even on locking bolts. Their uses shown here may spark other applications for the grape that has appeared in myriad art forms and since Bacchus was known in ancient times to be the Roman God of wine and intoxication.

Clip art. grapes.

Left:
George Witzke. Gate element. Forged trellis and grapes, plasma cut leaves, and copper wire tendrils. Trellis is colored with copper sulphate, and leaves and grapes with Gilder's paste. *Photo, April Witzke*

John Barron. Grapes on a branch for a wine rack. *Photo, Keith Sutter*

Jerry R. Spiker. Purple grapes on a textured vine. *Photo, artist*

Robert Wiederrick. Grape clusters, leaves, and tendrils become the focal theme for a fireplace screen. *Photo, Michelle Wiederrick*

Butch Lee. Grape leaf cluster, vines, and leaves used on a staircase railing. *Photo, David Harris*

46

Robb Gunter. Light fixture for a master room with grapes, vines, and stylized birds. *Photo, artist*

George Witzke. Slide bolt with grape cluster handle used for a wine cellar door. 4" high, 13" wide. *Photo, April Witzke*

Rob Gardner and Eric Velleca. Forged vines, laser cut forged leaves, forged grapes and tendrils for a wine storage room door. *Photo, Ken Nelson*

Robert C. Bentley. Two grape clusters are wrapped around a newspaper box in front of a private residence. *Photo, Bruce Woodworth*

Robert C. Bentley. Detail of the grape cluster with the leaves and vine. Finish is oil rubbed colors and acrylics. *Photo, Bruce Woodworth*

Jeff Holtby. Grape cluster created with a specially made spring die made for a power hammer. *Photo, Rachel Olsson*

Debra Turner. Grapes made from ball bearings hammered to achieve different lengths and textures. *Photo, Eric Montgomery*

Jeff Fetty. Forged steel grapevine for the window grille of a café. *Photo, Gefeti*

Vines and Leaves

Leaves, too, are expressed in iron. They lend themselves to elongated forms that can accompany bars and scrolls on gates, fences, and railings. Though they are often used in conjunction with flowers and grape clusters, it's fascinating to see how they are used and where.

Large leaves and leaf clusters are frequently used for gates, and especially where the bottom of the gate must form a barrier to small animals. In using leaves, the ironworker often becomes an amateur botanist studying the types of leaves that will work well for a particular project.

The type of leaves used can also indicate the territory or climate for which the gate or fence will be used. In desert countries, yucca leaves may dominate. In certain western states, aspen leaves may be popular and used on fireplace screens and lighting fixtures. Oak leaves may be used for detailing a mid-western home that also uses oak wood furniture.

Leaves also provide the metal worker with an opportunity to play with his artistry by seeing how they are textured, how colored, and the materials that may be combined.

Left:
George Witzke. Yucca plant with pods used on a gate. *Photo, April Witzke*

Above:
George Witzke. Close-up of fold-formed copper pods on a gate featuring yucca cactus. *Photo, April Witzke*

George Witzke. Grapes and leaves become part of a mirror frame. *Photo, April Witzke*

Helmut Hillenkamp. Detail on a gate. *Photo, artist*

John Boyd Smith. Leaves with thistles. *Photo, Rhonda Neil Fleming*

Robert Wiederrick. Aspen leaves are part of a fireplace screen. *Photo, Michelle Wiederrick*

Jack Brubaker. Leaves, flowers, and tendrils create a composition in a circle. Leaves are veined and the edges resemble a piecrust rim. *Photo, artist*

Right:
John Barron. Corner turn with leaves and collaring for the "owl" handrail (see page 90). *Photo, Keith Sutter*

Steve Lopes. Dining room chandelier with leaves, candles, and electric lights. *Photo, Craig Wester*

Lars Stanley. Various leaves clustered and carefully arranged for the
Zilker Botanical Garden Gate, Austen, Texas. *Photo, Atelier Wong*

Richard Prazen. Oak leaves and acorns adorn a banquette light fixture. The frame is heavily striated. *Photo, artist*

John Schneider. Leaf used as part of an end table décor. *Photo, artist*

61

Chapter 3

Critters with Character

Critters of many sizes may be formed using hand tools or power hammers. Small ones are usually forged from rods or bars; often they are made from soft metals such as copper and brass. Larger ones may be made of metal plate using repoussé methods.

Small critters, under 12 inches, and perhaps only 2- 6" long are used for detailing on gates, railings, fireplace screens, curtain rods, and door pulls. Larger ones may be made for light fixtures, or public art indoors and out.

Look for them at childrens' zoos, art museums, gardens, playgrounds, and amusement parks. They may appear as small sculptures or large sculptures to introduce a themed ride or play area. Some may be used on weather vanes that may depict a story from a well-known nursery rhyme.

Figures of animals and people are popular for fireplace screens that become as important a work of art in a home as a wall painting. Scenes, people's hobbies and special interests, symbols, and even stories of events are visually related in these personalized and customized screens. And they do require the best artistic talents of the metal worker.

The objects shown illustrate the potential of the medium, how figures are used, and provide ideas for decorators and artists.

Left:
Helmut Hillenkamp. Smoky dragon head spits both fire and water. It was installed on a sculpture body created in Cuenca, Ecuador, as public art on the Dragon Plaza. Head is 6 ft. long. *Photo, Fausto Cardoza*

Kirk Sullens. Jaguar for a chandelier for the Bass Pro Shop, Grapevine, Texas. The yellow color is hot brushed brass patina, the black spots are colored marker. *Photo, artist*

Kirk Sullens. Jaguar for a chandelier, front view. *Photo, artist*

Kirk Sullens. Water buffalo for the chandelier for the Bass Pro Shop, Grapevine, Texas. Power wire brushing, and then heating almost to a grey heat resulted in the blue-black patina. *Photo, artist*

Todd Caffo. Dog's head. Mild steel. 4" long, 3" wide, 3" high. *Photo, JoAnne Palasi*

Kirk Sullens. Moose for above a fireplace door for the Finger Lakes, New York, Bass Pro shop. Drawings show details for the scene behind the moose. 14" high. *Photo, artist*

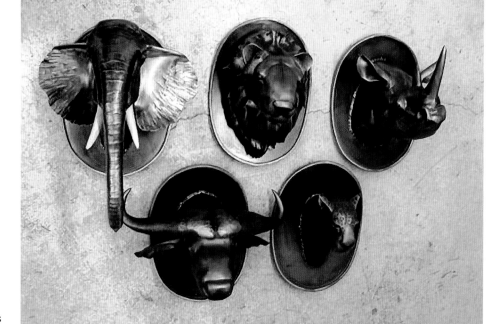

Left:
Kirk Sullens. Elephant head for the chandelier. *Photo, artist*

Kirk Sullens. Africa's Big 5 game animals made for a chandelier for the fine gunroom of the Bass Pro Shop, Grapevine, Texas. *Photo, artist*

Robert Wiederrick. Mother bear with cub, on a fireplace screen. *Photo, Michelle Wiederrick*

Right, top:
Robert Wiederrick. Elk detail on a fire screen. *Photo, Michelle Wiederrick*

Right, bottom:
Kirk Sullens. Fox. *The Color of Wheat* Medallion. *Photo, artist*

Robert Wiederrick. Beaver gnawing on the fire screen's frame. *Photo, Michelle Wiederrick*

Robert Wiederrick. Bear detail on a fire screen. *Photo, Michelle Wiederrick*

Mindy Gardner. Dog with ear detail showing the repoussé and raising textural effects.
Photo, artist

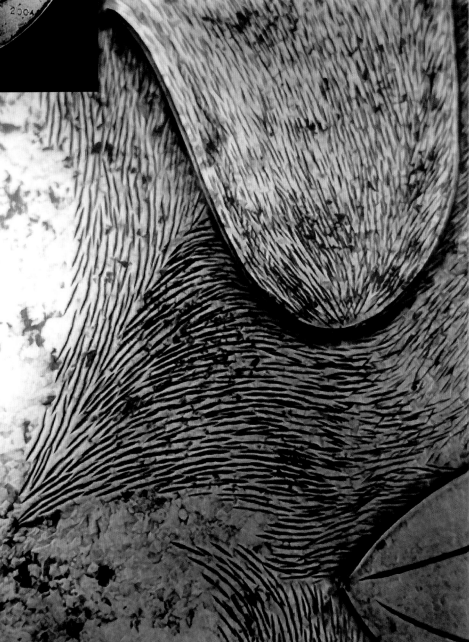

Ear detail.

John Boyd Smith. Pheasant fire screen. *Photo,
Rhonda Neil Fleming*

John Boyd Smith. Eagle feeding its
eaglets on a fire screen. Photo,
Rhonda Neil Fleming

72

John Boyd Smith. Dog fire screen.
Photo, Rhonda Neil Fleming

Glenn F. Gilmore. Copper inset for a fire screen with a repoussé dog's head. *Photo, McNabb Studio*

73

Robert Wiederrick. Buffalo Hunt fire screen certainly tells a story. *Photo, Michelle Wiederrick*

Robert Wiederrick. Flying duck fire screen.
Photo, Michelle Wiederrick

Robert Wiederrick. Second side of buffalo hunt fire screen. *Photo, Michelle Wiederrick*

Robert Wiederrick. Stainless steel flying heron fire screen. *Photo, Michelle Wiederrick*

Robert Wiederrick. Fish on a wood door. *Photo, Michelle Wiederrick*

Robert Wiederrick. Rainbow trout with a mayfly, on a fire screen. *Photo, Michelle Wiederrick*

Jim Sage. Three dimensional fish using an inflation technique with 20 gauge sheet metal. Two sides of the fish are cut and details, such as eyes and fins, are punched. The halves are edge welded with oxyacetylene gas and a mild steel filler rod. An in-flow pipe is inserted in the fish mouth and an out-flow pipe with a shutoff valve is welded in the vent area of the fish. The in-flow pipe is connected to a pressure washer and, when all the air is purged from the fish, the valve on the out-flow pipe is slowly closed. The resulting hydraulic pressure then forms the fish into a three-dimensional object. *Photos, Michael Sangster*
Top to bottom: Viper fish, Spotted Perch, Gar fish.

John Boyd Smith. Details of sea creatures form the base of a marine motif table. *Photo, Rhonda Neil Fleming*

Chuck Wall. Detail of one side of a lantern with fish for use in a seafood restaurant. Steel and copper. 22" high. *Photo, Kirk Sullens*

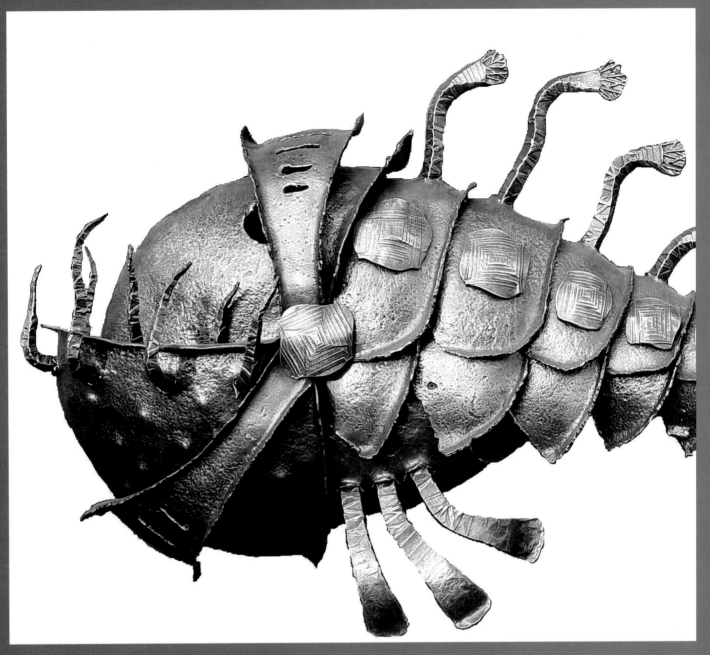

Vadim Filatov and Alexander Chumakov. Gvozd Studio. Gladiator fish armor. From an 18" sculpture, below. *Photos, artist*

Gladiator Fish

Erin McNeal Flores. Snail used among flowers, vines, and other creatures, on a headboard. *Photo, Frank Brabec*

Toshi Kawai. Snail made with hand formed Damascus steel. *Photo, artist*

George Witzke. Bee of 1.25" pipe with antennae and legs of nails and wire. Used on a gate. *Photo, April Witzke*

Center left:
Helmut Hillenkamp. Giant tic, for a drapery rod. *Photo, artist*

Center right:
Rob Gardner and Eric Velleca. Butterfly at rest on a garden fence. *Photo, artists*

Left:
George Witzke. Turtle is an interior door pull of mild steel. 6" wide, 8" long. *Photo, April Witzke*

Kirk Sullens. *Octopus*. A sculpture. Earlier versions were made with hooks for hanging clothes. 8" diam. About 2 " high. *Photo, artist*

Chuck Wall. Copper octopus on a lantern. Glass by John Perkins. Made for a Florida seafood restaurant. 22" high. *Photo, Kirk Sullens*

George Witzke. Ant of steel pipe and nails. *Photo, April Witzke*

George Witzke. Ladybug is a towel ring of 1/4" steel plate cut in a 6" circle and shaped. The eyes are brass rivets. *Photo, April Witzke*

Robert Wiederrick. Owl on a fireplace screen. *Photo, Michelle Wiederrick*

Mike Joyce. Trilobite. Detail on a tree of life for the Cloud Cliff Bakery Café and Artspace, Santa Fe, New Mexico. *Photo, Helmut Hillenkamp*

Helmut Hillenkamp. Curtain rod holder with an owl for a private residence. *Photo, Joe Openheimer*

Jerry R. Spiker. (Left and above.) Hummingbirds with morning glories. Details used on a railing, extended wall sculpture, and matching drapery rod endings. *Photo, artist*

Kirk Sullens. Insects for a gate at the Disney Grand Californian Hotel. Butterfly. Pierced steel and brass sheet. Wingspan, 8" wide. *Photo, artist*

Kirk Sullens. Ant. Steel. 6" long. *Photo, artist*

Kirk Sullens. Caterpillar for a gate of the Disney Grand Californian Hotel. 3" overall.

Kirk Sullens. Dragon-fly. Steel. Approx. 8" wingspan.

Kirk Sullens. Preying Mantis. Insects for the gates. Approx. 6" wide.
Photos, artist

John Barron. Owl hovering over a theme staircase. *Keith Sutter*

Right:
John Barron. Mouse incorporated into the railing with the owl theme. *Photo, Keith Sutter*

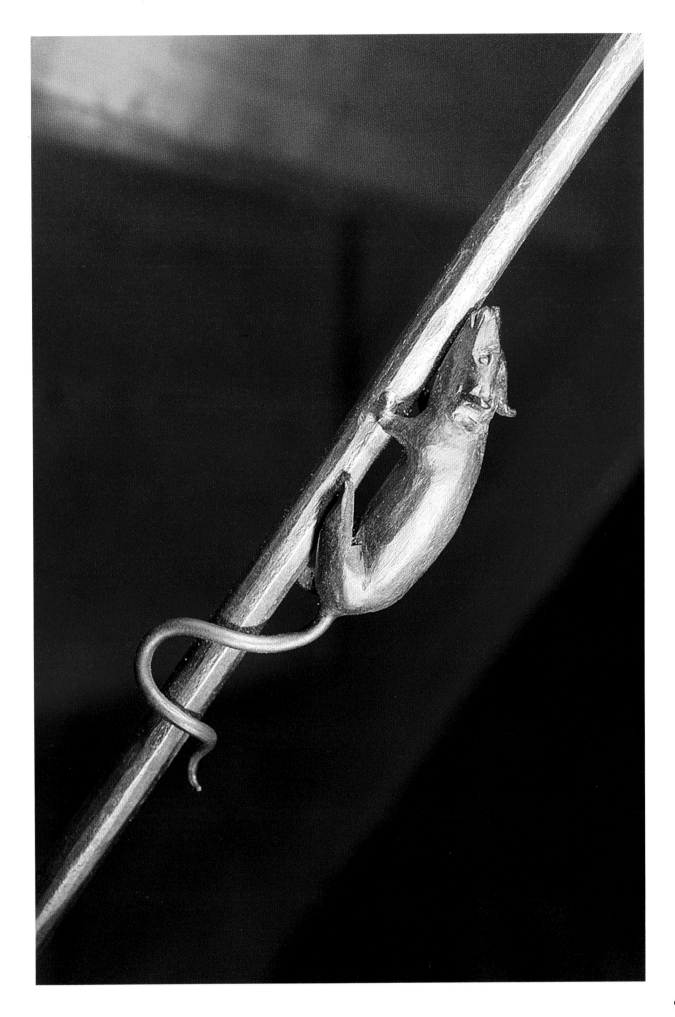

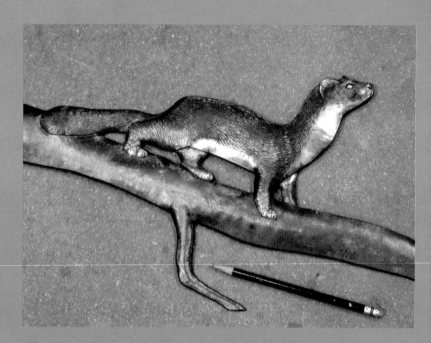

Kirk Sullens. Short tailed weasel, made to set in a decorative oval in a handrail, two sided but not fully 3 dimensional. Approx. 14" long. *Photo, artist*

George Parker. Scorpion on a window grille. About 4" long. *Photo, artist*

George Parker. Rattlesnake with fangs appears on a window grille. The snake's head is about 1.5" diam. *Photo, artist*

Tomás Arrey. Dragon from the gate of the Cloudcliff Bakery Café and Art Space, Santa Fe, New Mexico. *Photo, Helmut Hillenkamp*

Neil B. Mansfield. *Drago Volant.* Flying dragon made from 1.5" stock with bronze horns, copper tongue, and wings. Wings are repoussé. 19" long. *Photo, artist*

Joe Delaronde. Ram's head from the gate of the Cloudcliff Bakery Café and Art Space, Santa Fe, New Mexico. *Photo, Helmut Hillenkamp*

John Prosser. Colorado Big Horn sheep for the gates of the Cloudcliff Bakery Café and Art Space, Santa Fe, New Mexico. *Photo, Helmut Hillenkamp*

Vadim Filatov and Alexander Chumakov. Gvozd Studios. Dragon on a fire log holder. *Photo, artists*

John Morgan. A "king" from the gate of the Cloudcliff Bakery Café and Art Space, Santa Fe, New Mexico. *Photo, Helmut Hillenkamp*

John Boyd Smith. Ends of fire tools. *Photo, Rhonda Neil Fleming*

Jerry R. Spiker. Cowboys on branding rod handles. *Photo, artist*

Greg Eng. Bird with babies on a fire screen. *Photo, Brenda Eng*

Rob Gardner and Eric Velleca. Hare riding on a turtle; detail for a garden fence. *Photo, artists*

Robert Wiederrick. *After the Hunt* shows a tired horse and rider on a themed fire screen. *Photo, Michelle Wiederrick*

Todd Caffo. Horse's head. Steel. 4" long, 3" wide, 3" high. *Photo, JoAnne Palasi*

George Parker. Horse's head on a chandelier. 2" long. *Photo, artist*

Robert C. Bentley. Cast pewter Arabian horse head with frame. One of four located on "shear panels" for the main gates of a housing development. *Photo, Bruce Woodworth*

Daniel Miller. *Ariadne's Crown.* The central vertical bar has been punched and a horizontal bar drawn out and flattened. Collars couple the additional uprights. Full image of the sculpture. *Photo, Steven Keull*

Chapter 4

Joining:
Punching, Collaring,
and Riveting

It is often difficult to isolate individual techniques metalworkers use for joining one or more pieces to another. Often more than one procedure appears in any one section and throughout an entire piece. Railings, accessories, gates, all require that pieces be joined. Welding is a viable method, but it may not be as decorative and as permanent as one would hope. So additional methods developed by blacksmiths may be used to hide welded areas, and to make a joint stronger and more attractive.

These methods may include punching a hole in one piece and threading another piece through it. Collars, or bands, and rivets are used to join two or more pieces. Joinery methods may include mortise and tenon, pegging, and similar joinery often associated with woodworking.

Sometimes this joining is referred to as "coupling." Regardless of the title, the variants among these essential techniques are infinite. After viewing joinery details here, you will very likely begin observing joining methodology wherever iron appears. And it is all around you, in fences, gates, grilles, furniture, fireplace accessories, and lighting fixtures. As you become familiar with joinery techniques, also notice how those elements are finished…smooth, textured, hammered, raised, flat, rounded, and so forth. They are a clear expression of each smith's work and are almost as identifiable as a thumbprint.

George Parker. Contrasting colors for collaring add interest and conceal the welds used for joining elements. *Photo, artist*

Daniel Miller. *The Coupler's Will,* a wrought iron oil lamp. *Photo, Steven Keull*

Daniel Miller. Close up detail of *The Coupler's Will* illustrates several joining techniques; a hole is punched that allows another piece of iron to be drawn through. That piece is split and each side is bent back securing the horizontal to the vertical band. Square rivets are functional and decorative. *Photo, Steven Keull*

Robert Young. Detail of the central element of the table below. Punched areas, rivets, and collars are used for functional and decorative details. *Photos, Tom Mills*

Robert Young. Table, showing the placement and use of the detailed central element.

Daniel Smith. Reverse flower detail. Folded angle iron forge welded and riveted. *Photo, Polly Chandlers*

Walt Hull. Detail from a reredos behind the altar of a church using riveted stacked bars. *Photo, Wally Emerson*

Richard Schrader. Maquette for a railing with different sized collars, scroll ends, and twisted uprights. *Photo, artist*

Jeff Holtby. Table detail. The collar itself is detailed. *Photo, Rachel Olsson*

Zachary Noble. Andirons detail. Punching and riveting. *Photo, Tom Mills*

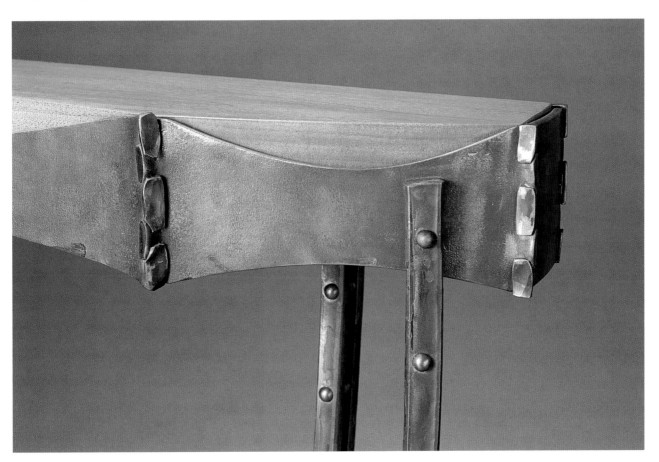

Robert Young. Table detail with rivets and support ends carefully upset so they appear as thumb prints and look soft despite the hardness of the metal. *Photo, Tom Mills*

Susan Madacsi. Fireplace detail. Decorative rivets. The protruding ends have been upset…meaning the metal is hammered back onto itself while it is heat softened. *Photo, R. J. Phil*

David Browne. Handle detail for a tray. *Photo, Jo Ann Palasi*

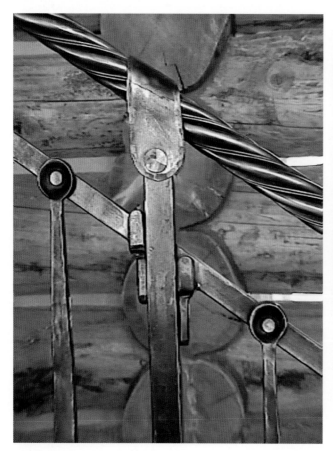

Smyth Boone. Riveted wrapped pieces hold a twisted bar for a railing. *Photo, artist*

Smyth Boone. Torch with rivets of different sizes and shapes. *Photo, artist*

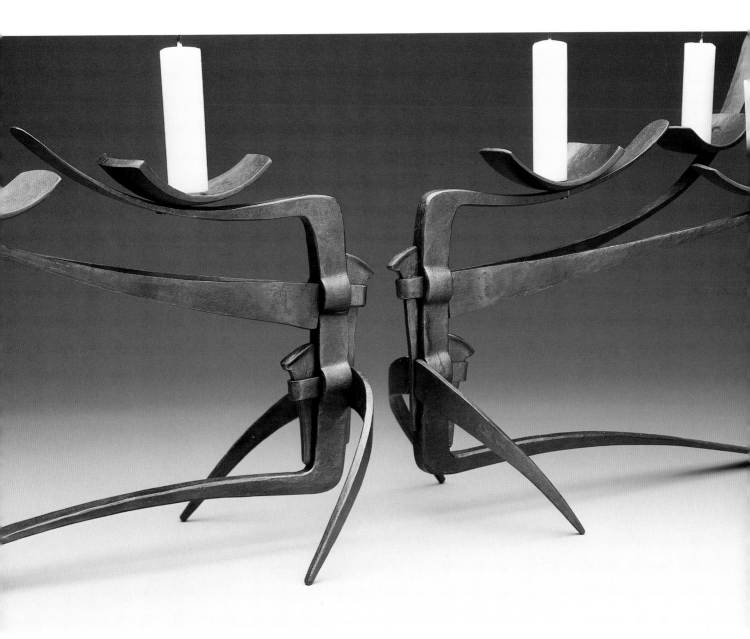

Daniel Miller. Viewing this piece in its entirety is needed to appreciate the subtle and fluid use of joinery including punching, collaring, and riveting. *Photo, Steven Kuell*

Andrew Marlor. Details from a dog gate show how punched holes in the horizontal accommodate vertical bars that have been hammer textured on the top. *Photo, artist*

Nikolay Seminov. Collaring and riveting for the gate of St. Chapel along with the handle and lock. *Photo, artist*

Christopher Thomson. Garden Gate joinery and latch. *Photo, Peter Vitale*

Robert C. Bentley. Steel with brass joinery of rivets, nuts, and screws. *Photo, Bruce Woodworth*

Jeff Holtby. Lever door lock with punching and riveting *Photo, Don Wodjienski*

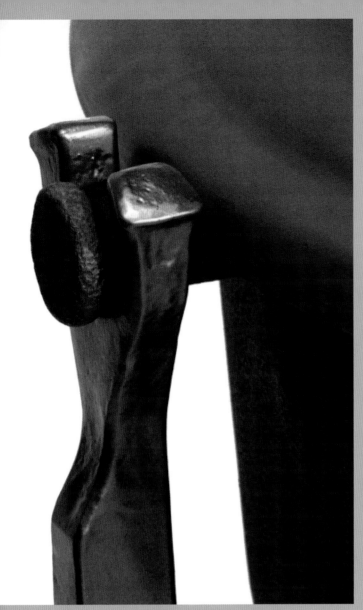

Jeff Holtby. Cauldron handles use a split bar with upset top ends, and a round bar within so the cauldron can be tipped for pouring. *Photo, Lynne Hann*

Jeff Holtby. Table base detail showing punching, riveting, and collaring. *Photo, David Gignac*

Nikolay Semenov. Collaring detail for a railing. *Photo, artist*

Sergey Sakirkin.
Collaring around rods
bent to form a corner
around a vertical bar.
Photo, artist

Bill Wilhelm. Scrolls collared to a frame. The frame was cut with a slitting chisel and the collar inserted for a unique variation on a traditional technique. *Photo, Walt Hester*

Nikolay Seminov. Collaring for a railing. *Photo, artist*

Daniel Miller. A forged iron brace is cleverly joined for use with a marble sculpture. *Photo, Steven Kuell*

R. Scott Oliver. Joinery for a table leg in different materials yields an appealing and functional detail. *Photo, Brian Jackson*

Stephen Marks. Moongate hinge details show the peg construction that joins moving elements. *Photo, William P. Wright*

Robert C. Bentley. Central element for a large conference table at the Villa Toscana uses mainly rivets and welding. *Photo, Bruce Woodworth*

Robert C. Bentley. Uprights are inset into the horizontal bars as supports for a railing. *Photo, Bruce Woodworth*

Chapter 5

Wraps and Scrolls

Just as joinery techniques are varied within any one project, so are wraps, and scrolls. Wrapping is similar to collaring…but collaring uses wide bands where wrapping suggests thinner strands holding other elements together. When you think of wrapping a bundle with twine the process is quick and you tie a knot and that's it. But when wrapping with thin strands of metal, the metals must be heated because hard metals can only be wrapped while they are heat softened. If thin, more malleable strips are used, the metal must be tempered so it doesn't break as it is manipulated.

Different colored metals, such as brass and copper, may be used for wrapping as well as collaring to introduce another color and design detail to a grille or railing. Thus it functions to join elements, hide a weld, add visual interest, and another surface dimension.

Scrolls are a basic element of decorative ironwork with shapes, sizes, textures, dimensions, and interaction endless. Scrolls, and their accompanying curves, may appear in single shapes, in multiples, in forward and backward combinations and they may be incorporated into leaves and other shapes. The ends may also be infinitely varied from narrow to wide, blunt to sharp, pointed or curved.

Smyth Boone. Scrolls simulate leaves. *Photo, artist*

Left:
Walt Hull. Detail of wrapping used on a large garden gate at a vineyard. *Photo, Wally Emerson*

Craig Kaviar.
Wrapped group of
bent textured
uprights for the table
base shown above.
Photo, artist

John Medwedeff. Metal wrapped around a console table leg. In both, note the collaring as joinery. *Photo, artist*

Elizabeth Brim. Tuffet, detail. A replica of a hassock with folds that simulate fabric using an inflation technique. *Photo, Tom Mills*

Walt Hull. Scroll detail with a leaf, and also showing punching, and riveting in one small section of a pedestrian gate.
Photo, Wally Emerson

Walt Hull. Wrapping and a tiny scroll for a garden gate. *Photo, Wally Emerson*

Walt Hull. Wrapping is both decorative and functional. The upright end is upset but then it is worked into a bud-like shape for heightened interest. *Photo, Wally Emerson*

Left and above:
Frederic A. Crist. Three Totems. Multiple steel wraps hot forged. Sculpture and detail. 92" high, 26" wide, 16" deep. *Photo, artist*

Susan Madacsi. Intricately wrapped joinery and uprights with upset ends. *Photo, R.J. Phil*

Matt Haugh. Scrolls have been elongated and shaped. Yet two tiny scrolls are used as decorative endings for the larger ones. Detail from a grille titled, *Square Dance. Photo, artist*

Larry Crawford. Fire screen with scrolls, flowers, leaves, and a horse. One of two panels.
Photo, Brenda Ladd

Sergey Sakirkin with **Schram.** A medley of scrolls with acanthus leaves and rosettes in forged steel and brass for a balcony rail. Joinery is collaring and rivets. *Photo, artist*

Stephen E. Lee. Scrolls incorporate leaf shapes for a residential decorative railing. *Photo, Kate Hoover*

Sergey Sakirkin. Wide scroll that gets even wider at the ends for the base of a large table. Four pieces are bound together by a collar and rivet. *Photo artist*

Stephen Marks. Wrapping joins flat sections, twists, and scrolls for a staircase. *Photo, William P. Wright*

Sergey Sakirkin. Scrolls, textured and smooth, curved and twisted, are major components of a railing. *Photo, artist*

Vadim Filatov and Alexander Chumakov. Gvozd Studios. Wrapped areas for a sculptural room divider in a clothing store. *Photo, artist*

Sergey Sakirkin. Scrolls within scrolls and other awesome detailing in a staircase. *Photo, artist*

Stephen E. Lee. Ovals with scrolls drawn to pointed ends course along the top and bottom of a stair rail. *Photo, Kate Hoover*

Roberta Elliott. Wrapping and scrolls. *Photo, Jeff Bruce*

David Browne. Detail from a candle holder with wrapping. *Photo, Jo Anne Palasi*

Andrew Marlor. Tapered spiral. *Photo, artist*

George Witzke. Chain with tightly wrapped coils used as an accessory to a mirror in a scroll design. *Photo, April Witzke*

George Witzke. Twisted iron wrapped and tied into a knot used as part of a sconce holder. *Photo, April Witzke*

John Medwedeff. Scrolls from *The Gately Arch. Photo, artist*

Robert C. Bentley. Scrolls become decorative support brackets for a large light fixture. *Photo, Bruce Woodworth*

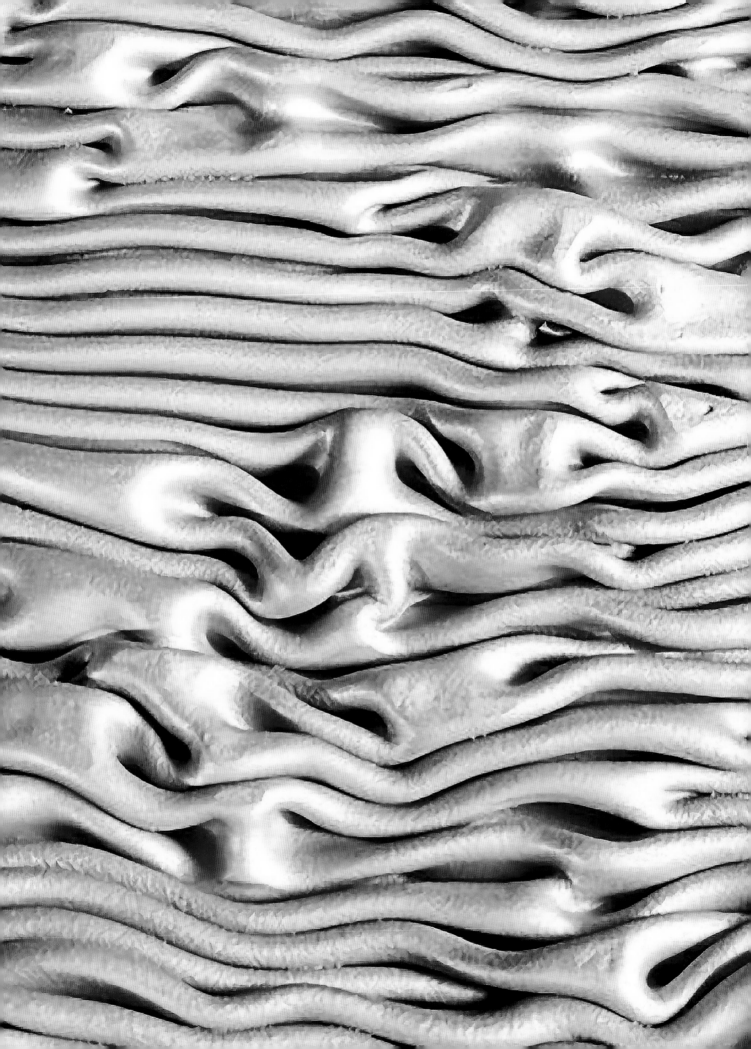

Chapter 6

Textures, Twists, Folds, and Weaves

Among the qualities of steel used for artwork is its ability to accommodate infinite textures. Most obvious are the patterns, or free form bumps and dents left from the force of the hammer on the metal. Pronounced hammer marks alone can change the surface of a piece of steel into a texture that is visually and tactilely pleasing.

Applying different shaped tools, heating, punching, folding, twisting, and weaving, can also produce scores of other textures. Only one's tools and imagination combined with trial and errors limit the effects possible. Adding acids, colorants, allowing the metal to rust when used outdoors, even painting the surfaces, all yield excitement.

Just the juxtaposition of different metal combinations creates color and texture interest. The reader is encouraged to go through the earlier chapters and observe textures and the many ways they may have been created.

Folds that simulate fabric or draperies are difficult to create in hard metals that must be softened and hammered to make them bend to the artist's vision. Yet the adept metal worker can make these hard materials appear as soft and textured as linen or leather.

Whitney Potter creates various textured samples in steel and copper for different projects. He says, "If a picture is worth a thousand words, a sample is surely worth many thousand. No drawing or photograph can convey to a client the tactile nature of forged iron. I like to hand a client a sample bar and say this is what your piece will look like, and this is what it will feel like. These textures are made with a power hammer using simple shop built dies."

Russell Jaqua. Privacy gate, detail. *Photo, David Conklin*

Left:
Whitney Potter. Detail of a convoluted copper vessel forged under a hydraulic press. *Photo, artist*

Enrique Vega. Twisted bar patterns can differ tremendously depending upon the size and configuration of a bar as well as the direction and depth of the twist. *Photo, artist*

Jerry R. Spiker. Textured pipes for floral vines, grape vines, morning glory vines, etc. *Photo, artist*

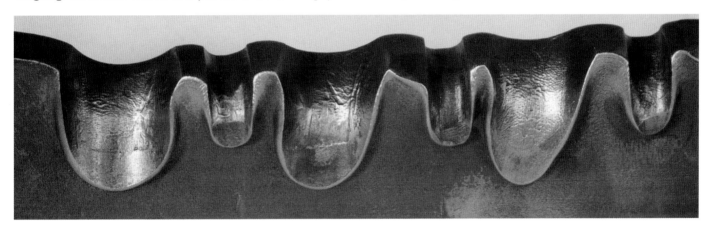

Greg Eng. Twisted bars used for door pulls and trim around large pot racks. *Photo, Brenda Eng*

Whitney Potter. Gouged bar. Sample. *Photo, artist*

George Witzke. Abstract bar made from a piece of 1" stock and hammered repetitively off the corners of flat dies using a power hammer. *Photo, April Witzke*

Jeff Fetty. Table leg using squished pipe. *Photo,Gefeti*

Whitney Potter. Squishy pipe 2. Detail of a floor lamp made from steel pipe squished under a hydraulic press. *Photo, artist*

Dan Nauman. Textured hanging devices with twists and curves based
on a historical light fixture by Cyril Colnik. *Photo, Peter Lottermoser*

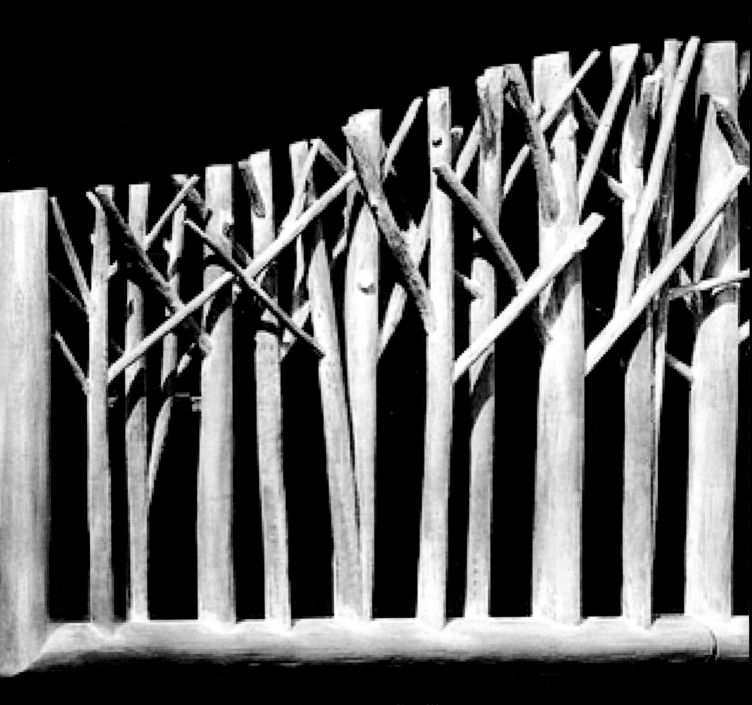

Weimann Iron Works. Treegate. Iron is simulated to look like trees for a gate. *Photo, Weimann*

Left:
Michael Bendele. Wine bottle holder with different twists. *Photo, artist*

Amy Winkel. A wall plaque with various textures incorporates repoussé, hammer marks, and acids. *Photo, Cheryl Brodie*

Joan Waters. From a *Scarification Series, Amber*. Welded, textured steel with patinas. Any detailed portion of this sculpture yields a variety of texture examples. 42" high, 21" wide, 9" deep. *Photo, artist*

Vadim Filatov and Alexander Chumakov. Gvozd Studios. Folded shapes that represent fabric and ribbon details in a clothing store railing. *Photo, artists*

Helmut Hillenkamp. Top of a fence post with curved back loops coming to a point. *Photo, artist*

Mecki Heussen. Bamboo simulated in iron using a specially designed press. *Photo, artist*

Paul Cheney. Basket weave detail from a wall sculpture. *Photo, artist*

Robert Wiederrick. Fire screen with woven detail. *Photo, Michelle Wiederrick*

David Browne. Fire screen with woven detail. *Photo, JoAnn Palesi*

Robert Wiederrick. Fire screen with woven detail. *Photo, Michelle Wiederrick*

153

Whitney Potter. Copper and steel lighting sconce detail. *Photo, artist*

Robert C. Bentley. California Mission kick panel plate on main entry gate of the Santa Ysabel Ranch, Paso Robles, California. Cast aluminum relief painted a bronze color. One of 16 panels comprising a theme. *Photo, Bruce Woodworth*

Russell Jaqua. Security fence and detail shows the texture on the face and edge of each overlapped panel. At the bottom is the full fence. *Photo, David Conklin*

Weimann Iron Works. Rococo fire and security doors of cast bronze. *Photo, courtesy Weimann*

Index